Original title:

The Framework of Friendship

Copyright © 2024 Swan Charm
All rights reserved.

Author: Sara Säde
ISBN HARDBACK: 978-9916-86-563-7
ISBN PAPERBACK: 978-9916-86-564-4
ISBN EBOOK: 978-9916-86-565-1

Roots and Wings

Deep in the earth, our roots spread wide,
Anchoring dreams where hope abides.
Reaching so high, we dare to fly,
With every gust, we touch the sky.

Yet still we cherish the soil's embrace,
Where love is sown in timeless space.
Together we grow, both strong and free,
Bound by the past, yet wild as the sea.

Melodies of Togetherness

In harmony's glow, our voices align,
Strings of connection, forever entwined.
Each note we share, a story unfolds,
A tapestry woven with threads of gold.

Through laughter and tears, our song finds its way,
Echoing moments that brightly display.
Together we dance, through troubles and cheer,
In the symphony of life, you are always near.

Lanterns in the Dark

In shadowed nights, our lanterns glow,
Guiding each step, through joy and woe.
With flickering flames, we light the way,
Chasing the fears that dare to stay.

Each spark a promise, a beacon of hope,
Illuminating paths where we learn to cope.
Together we shine, bright against the night,
With love as our lantern, we find the light.

Mosaic of Memories

Pieces of laughter, shards of our past,
Forming a picture, built to last.
Each memory colored, vibrant and clear,
A mosaic of moments held so dear.

From whispers of youth to dreams yet untold,
We gather our stories like treasures of gold.
In the heart of our journey, these fragments we share,
Creating a masterpiece, beyond compare.

Tides of Trust

In whispers soft, the sea does swell,
With every wave, a tale to tell.
Trust builds like sand, with time it flows,
In gentle tides, our friendship grows.

Through stormy nights and sunny days,
We ride the waves in countless ways.
Anchored deep, our hearts align,
With every tide, our souls entwine.

Bonds Carved in Time

Like rivers carve through ancient stone,
Our bonds grow strong, never alone.
In moments shared, we find our way,
Together we shine, come what may.

Time weaves threads of silver bright,
In laughter's glow and sorrow's night.
Each memory etched, forever clear,
A tapestry rich, my friend, so dear.

Heartstrings Entwined

In melodies sweet, our hearts do sing,
With every note, pure love takes wing.
Entwined like roots that dig so deep,
In trust we blossom, no secrets to keep.

Through trials faced and moments shared,
Our heartstrings dance, beautifully paired.
With gentle hands, we weave our fate,
Together we'll thrive, let love create.

Gathered Moments

In pockets deep, we keep our dreams,
Gathered moments, like flowing streams.
Each laugh and tear, a treasure rare,
In life's great book, we find our share.

Through seasons change, we stand as one,
Collecting warmth from the rising sun.
In every heartbeat, memories stay,
Gathered moments, come what may.

Shared Laughter

In the warm glow of twilight,
Friends gather, spirits bright.
Echoes of joy fill the air,
Laughter dances, light as air.

Stories woven in playful jest,
Hearts united, we feel blessed.
Each chuckle draws us near,
Moments cherished, crystal clear.

Breezes carry our delight,
Memories sparkling in the night.
Together we create a song,
In this bond, we all belong.

Bridges of Understanding

Two worlds meet on common ground,
In shared silence, we are found.
Eyes speak truths we all know,
Building bridges, letting flow.

With every step, we dare to share,
Opening hearts, laying bare.
In the warmth of the embrace,
We discover a sacred space.

Through storms of life, we see light,
In shadows, we find our might.
Hands entwined, we walk as one,
A journey forged, just begun.

Illuminated Connections

Stars twinkle in the vast expanse,
Each one holds a tale, a chance.
Silent whispers in the dark,
Illuminated paths we embark.

Through the laughter and the tears,
We weave a tapestry of years.
Threads of hope interlace,
In the fabric of time and space.

Light shines from eyes sincere,
Guiding us, year after year.
In every hug, a spark ignites,
Illuminated connections, a lantern in the nights.

Roots of Loyalty

Deep in the earth, our roots entwine,
In whispered promises, we align.
Through storms and seasons, we stand strong,
Bound by trust, where we belong.

With every challenge, side by side,
In unity, we choose to abide.
Faithful hearts, steadfast and true,
In this loyalty, we both grew.

As time unfolds, we bloom anew,
In a garden, rich with hues.
Through the ups and downs, we remain,
Roots of loyalty, a sacred chain.

Reflections in Each Other

In the mirror of your eyes,
I see my dreams take flight,
Your laughter is the sun,
That warms my lonely night.

In whispered thoughts we share,
Our hopes begin to blend,
With every glance we take,
Our hearts begin to mend.

Like shadows dancing close,
In twilight's gentle glow,
We hold what cannot fade,
In love's soft afterglow.

Together we unite,
In the silence that we keep,
With you, I find my strength,
In moments vast and deep.

In reflections, we discover,
The paths our lives will trace,
Two souls in harmony,
In this sacred space.

Communal Echoes

Voices rise like gentle waves,
In the stillness of the night,
We gather in the twilight,
Our dreams take graceful flight.

Hands intertwined like roots,
We weave a tapestry,
Every heart a thread,
In our shared symphony.

The echoes of our laughter,
Bounce off the distant walls,
In unity we stand,
While each spirit calls.

Beneath the stars we thrive,
In stories yet untold,
Finding strength together,
More precious than pure gold.

With every step we take,
Our journey feels complete,
In the chorus of our lives,
Where strangers turn to meet.

A Symphony of Souls

Each note a heartbeat played,
In this grand design,
Together we create,
A rhythm pure and fine.

The melody we share,
Carries us through time,
With harmonies we rise,
In life's sweet, sacred rhyme.

In moments filled with grace,
Our dreams begin to swell,
Each whisper forms a song,
That only we can tell.

With every chord we strike,
The world begins to dance,
In the beauty of the now,
We find our second chance.

Together we compose,
This timeless, vibrant tune,
A symphony of souls,
Where love is always in bloom.

Gathering of Hearts

Beneath a sky of stars,
Our laughter fills the air,
A gathering of souls,
With stories that we share.

In circle, hand in hand,
We find our common ground,
Each heartbeat echoes softly,
In love's embrace, we're bound.

Through seasons of our lives,
The bonds of trust we weave,
In every smile exchanged,
We learn how to believe.

With every tear we've known,
And every joy we greet,
We celebrate this journey,
With hearts that skip a beat.

Together we will rise,
In this dance of the brave,
A gathering of hearts,
In memories we save.

Harmonies of Heartfelt Moments

In the soft glow of twilight's hue,
We whisper dreams, just me and you.
Each heartbeat sings a timeless song,
In every glance, where we belong.

Moments gather like stars in the night,
With every laugh, our spirits ignite.
Footsteps dance on the path we tread,
In the garden of memories, love is fed.

Through gentle breezes, memories sway,
Hand in hand, we greet the day.
Hope unfurls like petals in spring,
In the silence, our souls take wing.

Beneath the moon's serene embrace,
We find our refuge, our sacred space.
Soft whispers weave through shadows cast,
In the light of love that forever lasts.

Adventures in Togetherness

With every step, we brave the wild,
Side by side, forever a child.
The world unfolds, a canvas bright,
In your laughter, I find my light.

Through winding paths and whispers low,
Together we trace the tales we know.
Each journey dear, a treasure trove,
In the dance of hearts that gently rove.

From sunrise dreams to sunset's kiss,
With every moment, we find our bliss.
In laughter shared and tears unveiled,
Our spirits soar, our love shall not pale.

We sail on waves of boundless delight,
Exploring the stars that twinkle bright.
Through the storms and the sunlit days,
In your arms, my heart forever stays.

Threads of Time

In the tapestry of days gone by,
We weave together, you and I.
With threads of joy and colors bright,
We stitch the moments, love's pure light.

The hours whisper secrets near,
In every laughter, in every tear.
Time's gentle hand does softly twine,
Our hearts entwined, like sacred wine.

Memories linger, scents of the past,
In the embrace of moments that last.
We hold each thread with tender care,
In the fabric of love that we both share.

As seasons change and rivers flow,
In every heartbeat, our love shall grow.
Together we journey through life's grand rhyme,
Forever stitched in the threads of time.

Bonds Beyond Borders

In distant lands our hearts unite,
Across the seas, we share the light.
No matter where our dreams may roam,
Together we will find our home.

With every word, a bridge we build,
In every laugh, our souls are filled.
Beyond the lines that separate,
Our friendship, strong, will never wait.

From every corner, voices rise,
In harmony, we touch the skies.
A tapestry of colors bright,
Woven close, in timeless plight.

Together we can face the storm,
In unity, our hearts stay warm.
For in this bond, we rise above,
A world connected by our love.

Threads of Trust

In woven strands of truth we find,
A bond that time cannot unbind.
Each whispered secret shared in grace,
Builds a fortress, our sacred space.

Through trials faced, we stand as one,
With every test, our hearts have won.
A tapestry of stories spun,
In every thread, our trust begun.

Hand in hand, we journey through,
The darkest nights, the brightest blue.
We lift each other, light the way,
In threads of trust, we choose to stay.

The fabric of our lives entwined,
A bond so strong, forever kind.
In every stitch, a tale unfolds,
Of love and courage, never cold.

Echoes of Kindred Spirits

In the silence, whispers call,
From distant lands, we feel it all.
Our spirits dance, a sacred thread,
In every heartbeat, love is spread.

Like stars that shine in endless night,
Kindred souls, we share the light.
In laughter shared and tears that fall,
An echo rings, a timeless thrall.

Together in this cosmic play,
We find our paths, come what may.
In every moment, close we stand,
As kindred spirits, hand in hand.

Through stormy seas, we sail with grace,
Each wave, a part of our embrace.
In every voice, a melody,
Of love's sweet song, forever free.

Paths Intertwined

Two paths converge in twilight's glow,
With every step, the bond will grow.
In every choice, a thread we weave,
A story rich, we both believe.

With laughter echoing in the night,
In every dream, we chase the light.
Through winding roads and fields of gold,
Our journey shared, a tale retold.

Hand in hand, we face the rise,
The dawn of hope, beneath the skies.
In tangled roots, our strength does lie,
Together we will learn to fly.

In the moments, both small and grand,
We find our selves, we make our stand.
Paths intertwined, forever blessed,
In love's embrace, we are at rest.

Remnants of Reevaluation

In shadows deep, we ponder fate,
The echoes linger, love, and hate.
Reflections dance on waters still,
We seek the truth and bend to will.

What once was clear now fades away,
In twilight's grasp, we often stray.
Shattered thoughts in scattered light,
We find our way through endless night.

Moments lost, yet lessons gained,
Through trials harsh, our hearts unchained.
The past, a guide through tangled years,
We rise anew amidst our fears.

With open eyes, we dare to see,
The remnants left, the way to be.
In silent whispers, truth unfolds,
A tale of courage, brave and bold.

Glimpses of Gratitude

In morning's light, a soft embrace,
The world awakens, finds its grace.
Each fleeting moment, a gift to hold,
The heart remembers, stories told.

A smile exchanged, a hand to lend,
The ties that bind, we will defend.
Through trials faced, we stand as one,
Together stronger, battles won.

The gentle breeze, the rustling leaves,
With every breath, the spirit weaves.
In nature's wonder, joy is found,
We count our blessings, all around.

In quiet nights, we give our thanks,
For love that flows through all our ranks.
With open hearts, we seek to share,
Gratitude's light, a precious flare.

The Fire of Fellowship

Around the flame, we gather near,
In warmth and laughter, we share cheer.
With stories woven, bonds are spun,
Together shining, brighter than sun.

In shared dreams, our hopes entwine,
A tapestry of love, divine.
Through trials faced, our spirits soar,
In unity, we find much more.

The fire crackles, sparks take flight,
Illuminating the darkest night.
In every glance, a promise made,
With hearts ablaze, we won't evade.

Through storms we weather, hand in hand,
In fellowship, we truly stand.
When shadows loom, we share our light,
A beacon glowing, pure and bright.

Notes of Nostalgia

In faded photographs, we glimpse the past,
Time's gentle hand, its shadows cast.
Whispers linger, soft and sweet,
Moments cherished, we hold discreet.

The laughter echoes through the years,
In every smile, a trace of tears.
We dance in memories, long and wide,
A melody of love, our hearts abide.

With every sunset, stories grow,
In twilight's glow, we come to know.
The bonds we forged, still linger strong,
In notes of nostalgia, we belong.

Through dreams we travel, hand in hand,
In timeless whispers, we take a stand.
For every memory carved in time,
A testament to love's sweet rhyme.

Footprints in Unity

Together we walk on this road,
Leaving our marks where we go.
Side by side, hand in hand,
In the story of life, we stand.

With each step, our spirits rise,
Reflecting hope in the skies.
In laughter shared, we thrive,
With unity, we come alive.

Through storms and sun, we stay strong,
In each other, we belong.
Our footprints blend, a dance of grace,
In every heart, there's a place.

Echoing dreams in a melody,
We celebrate our harmony.
Woven together, thread by thread,
In the tapestry of what we've said.

So let us walk on, hearts entwined,
In the path where love is blind.
For in our journey, we connect,
Footprints in unity, we reflect.

Crossing the Divide

Bridges built from word and deed,
Across the divide, we plant a seed.
With every heart, a story shared,
In humble grace, we're unprepared.

Differences fade in the light,
As we gather the strength to unite.
Voices mingling like a song,
In diversity, we all belong.

Step by step, we face our fears,
Wiping away the silent tears.
With every laugh, with every sigh,
Together we learn how to fly.

Hands extended, reaching wide,
In a world where we'll abide.
Together we stand, side by side,
In love and faith, we'll ride.

A tapestry woven with care,
Every thread shows we dare.
Crossing the divide, hearts aglow,
Together, we learn, together we grow.

Chords of Companionship

In the silence, a melody plays,
Resounding through our gentle days.
With every note, our laughter rings,
In the warmth, companionship brings.

A strum of hope, a beat of cheer,
In this rhythm, we draw near.
As we dance through life on a whim,
Each chord a promise, never dim.

With shared stories and whispered dreams,
We find the light in the seams.
Harmony bonds the souls of friends,
In unity, the music bends.

Through trials, our notes may clash,
Yet in the discord, pure joys splash.
Together we create, we compose,
In every challenge, our spirit grows.

So let us strum our hearts in tune,
In the bright glow of the moon.
With chords of love that never cease,
In companionship, we find our peace.

Timeless Connections

In the fabric of time, we weave,
Moments captured, never to leave.
With each heartbeat, we grow strong,
Timeless connections where we belong.

Echoes of laughter fill the air,
In shared journeys, we always care.
Through seasons that change and shift,
In every bond, there's a gift.

We hold the past, yet look ahead,
In every word that we've said.
The stars above, they brightly shine,
Guiding our steps, yours and mine.

As roots intertwine in the soil,
Together we weather the toil.
In timelessness, our spirits blend,
In memories, love has no end.

So here's to the ties that bind,
In every heart, love defined.
In the tapestry of life, we find,
Timeless connections, forever entwined.

Kaleidoscope of Kinship

In colors bright, we find our way,
A tapestry of love each day.
Through laughter shared and tears that fall,
Together we rise, we stand tall.

The bonds we weave, both strong and true,
Reflect the light in me and you.
With every twist, a new design,
In life's great dance, your hand in mine.

From childhood dreams to grown-up hopes,
We navigate the world's wide slopes.
Each memory, a precious gem,
In this kaleidoscope, we blend.

Through seasons change, we hold the thread,
In whispered words and stories said.
United hearts through thick and thin,
Our kinship's strength, where we begin.

So let us cherish every hue,
For in this world, it's me and you.
Together, we paint the skies divine,
In this kaleidoscope, forever shine.

Storms Weathered Together

In darkest nights, we faced the rain,
With hands held tight, we eased the pain.
The lightning flashed, yet here we stand,
With courage drawn from heart's command.

Through howling winds and thunder's roar,
We found a strength we can't ignore.
In every gust, in every shake,
Our bond gives way to no heartache.

Each storm that came, a test of will,
But side by side, we conquer still.
With laughter shared amidst the fright,
We soar together into the night.

When clouds disperse, the sun will gleam,
Together we rise, a potent dream.
In every drop, a story sown,
We weather storms, and we have grown.

So take my hand when thunder calls,
For in this love, we'll never fall.
Our hearts entwined, a steadfast tether,
We'll brave this life, storms weathered together.

Starry Nights and Shared Stories

Beneath the stars, our whispers float,
With tales of old, shared dreams we wrote.
The cosmos wide, a canvas bright,
In every twinkle, pure delight.

With every story, we stitch the night,
In laughter's glow, all feels so right.
From fire's warmth, our spirits rise,
To dance beneath the endless skies.

Each journey shared, a bond that grows,
Through winding paths and highs and lows.
These moments dear, forever kept,
In heart's embrace, no need for slept.

So gather close, let memories start,
A tapestry woven from the heart.
In starry nights, our spirits soar,
With shared stories, we crave for more.

Together here, under celestial seas,
We find our peace in every breeze.
As constellations weave their thread,
In shared stories, love is fed.

The Essence of Togetherness

In every smile, the light we share,
In moments rare, we show we care.
With open hearts and guiding hands,
The essence of love truly stands.

Through trials faced and joys embraced,
We've built a bond that won't be chased.
Together we laugh, together we cry,
In this embrace, we learn to fly.

From whispered dreams to hopeful plans,
In unity, our journey spans.
With every step, we carve our way,
In the dance of life, come what may.

So take my hand, we'll journey far,
In this togetherness, we are a star.
In every heartbeat, feel the grace,
The essence of love, our sacred space.

So let's celebrate this bond so true,
In all we do, it's me and you.
In this embrace that we possess,
We find the essence of togetherness.

Celestial Companions

Stars whisper secrets high,
Moonlight dances in the sky.
Galaxies twirl, lost in dreams,
Cosmic light, or so it seems.

Planets wander, hand in hand,
In the dark, a silent band.
Stardust trails, a path so bright,
Guiding souls through endless night.

Nebulas paint a vibrant hue,
Colors blend, a canvas new.
Together in this vast expanse,
Celestial bodies sway and prance.

Eons pass, yet still they shine,
A bond unbroken, pure design.
Through the void, they weave and sigh,
Celestial companions in the sky.

In the hush of the lunar glow,
Dreamers find their hearts aglow.
Restless spirits, seeking peace,
In the stars, their worries cease.

Hands Across Time

Fingers stretch through endless years,
Wiping away forgotten tears.
Touching hearts with every word,
Silent echoes, softly heard.

Pages turn, each tale a thread,
Stories written, lives we've led.
Bridges built with ink and rhyme,
Uniting souls across all time.

Moments captured, forever stay,
In memories that won't decay.
Hands held tight in fleeting past,
A promise made, forever last.

Time may change, yet love remains,
In gentle whispers, hope sustains.
Together bound, we learn to climb,
Two hearts reaching, hands across time.

In the stillness of the night,
Visions dance in soft moonlight.
Echoes of our shared design,
A tapestry of love divine.

The Bridge of Communication

Voices carry on the breeze,
Words like leaves upon the trees.
Messages flow like gentle streams,
Bridging gaps with shared dreams.

In the silence, hearts can speak,
Connections form, we dare to seek.
Thoughts unite in a sacred space,
Embracing every soul with grace.

Signals sent, a beacon's call,
In every whisper, we enthrall.
Distance fades, we find our way,
A bridge of love in bright array.

Conversations under starlit skies,
Where truth blooms and darkness dies.
Understanding flows like wine,
Uniting spirits, yours and mine.

So let us share what words can't say,
Build the bridge, come what may.
In every heartbeat, let us find,
The strands of hope that intertwine.

Collective Journeys

Each path we tread, a story told,
In laughter shared, in hands we hold.
Together through life's winding roads,
In every challenge, love explodes.

Mountains climb, and rivers cross,
Side by side, we'll bear the loss.
Through tangled woods, we find the light,
Our collective hearts take flight.

From distant shores to skies so wide,
In unity, we find our guide.
The journey shared, a precious gold,
In every moment, brave and bold.

With every step, we learn and grow,
In shadows deep, our spirits glow.
Through storms we dance, through calm we sing,
Collective journeys, together we bring.

As stars align, our dreams ignite,
With steadfast hearts, we reach new heights.
Together in this cosmic swirl,
In every heartbeat, love unfurls.

The Art of Being Together

In quiet moments, we share our breath, With warmth that lingers, a bond of depth. Laughter dances in the softest light, Together we find solace in the night.

Hands entwined as the world slips away, In the gentle hush where hearts can sway. Each glance a promise, each sigh a song, In this precious space, we both belong.

Memories painted on canvas so bright, A tapestry woven with threads of delight. In every heartbeat, a story unfolds, Together we cherish what love beholds.

A journey taken, side by side we roam, With every step, we build our home. In the art of together, we find our grace, In this sacred union, a warm embrace.

So let us linger in the softest now, In the sacred present, we make our vow. To celebrate moments, both big and small, In the art of being together, we have it all.

Paths Crossed

In the quiet dawn, our paths align, A fleeting glance, a spark divine. Footsteps echo on the ancient stone, Here in the meeting, we are not alone.

Woven together by fate's gentle hand, Stories shared in a far-off land. Each word a bridge, each smile a key, Unlocking the truth of who we can be.

With every twist, our journeys unfold, Secrets whispered, memories told. Like rivers merging, we flow as one, Paths crossed beneath the setting sun.

In the dance of life, we sway and glide, In unity's rhythm, we find our stride. The compass of fate, a guiding star, Together we travel, no matter how far.

So here's to the moments, the fleeting chance, To embrace this journey, to take a stance. For every path crossed leads to our song, In the tapestry of life, we both belong.

In the Company of Kindred Spirits

Under moonlit skies, we share our dreams, In the company of kindred spirits, we glean. Laughter echoes, a comfortable tune, With every heartbeat, we're lost in the swoon.

Weaving tales of joy and grief, Finding solace in each shared belief. A gathering of hearts that understand, Together we journey, hand in hand.

Moments of silence, a knowing glance, In the warmth of friendship, we take a chance. Each voice a thread in the fabric of time, In this sacred space, our souls can climb.

Through mountains high and valleys low, In each other's strength, we constantly grow. Surrounded by love, we feel so alive, In the company of spirits, we truly thrive.

So let's raise a toast to the roads we share, To the bonds that connect us, a love so rare. For in the embrace of kindred delight, We find our home under the stars at night.

Stories Interwoven

In whispered echoes, our stories combine, Threads of experience, yours and mine. Like woven fabric, rich and rare, Each moment cherished, we pause and share.

Underneath the stars, our pasts collide, In the dance of history, we take pride. With every chapter, we learn and grow, In the tapestry of life, love starts to flow.

Stories interwoven, a sacred embrace, In the warmth of memories, we find our place. Each laugh, each tear, a testament true, In the bond of our tales, I'm here with you.

Seasons may change, like pages turned, Yet the fire of friendship still brightly burns. In the art of sharing, we find our way, Together we navigate each passing day.

So let's write our stories, with love as our ink, In the book of our lives, forever we'll link. For in every word and each moment we save, Are the stories interwoven, our hearts engrave.

Bonded by Threads

In the quiet dusk we meet,
Silken hopes in every heartbeat.
Entwined paths of fate we share,
Soft whispers float in the air.

With each touch, our spirits merge,
Woven tight, we feel the surge.
Colors blend, a vibrant hue,
Together strong, we are not few.

Memory threads through time's embrace,
Interlaced in love's sweet grace.
A tapestry of trust we spin,
Through every loss, we seek to win.

Through storms faced, we stand so firm,
In every challenge, we will learn.
Bonded tightly, we will strive,
With every thread, we come alive.

As seasons change, we still remain,
Through joy and sorrow, hope, and pain.
A fabric rich, a story told,
In threads of warmth, we find our gold.

Weaving Souls Together

Fingers dance on strands, so fine,
Creating patterns, hearts align.
With gentle knots, we hold the space,
In every weave, we find our place.

Threads of laughter pull us near,
In every stitch, we share the cheer.
Colors bright in radiant hues,
Together weaving, we refuse to lose.

Through the loom of life's embrace,
We craft a bond time cannot erase.
Endless threads, the stories blend,
In every corner, we transcend.

As seasons shift, our fabric grows,
In unity, strength overflows.
Weaving dreams as one, we soar,
In every thread, we seek for more.

Through laughter's light and shadows deep,
In every weave, our love we keep.
Together, we're a masterpiece
In every stitch, we find our peace.

Pillars of Understanding

Upon the ground, we build our trust,
In every word, an iron crust.
Pillars strong, we rise and stand,
In open hearts, we make our band.

Through gentle talks and honest ways,
We light the path through endless days.
With every doubt, we find the solve,
In understanding, we evolve.

The roots run deep, the branches high,
In every glance, we touch the sky.
Moments shared, we hold them tight,
In fragile times, we find our light.

Through storms and calm, we learn to see,
With every voice, we find the key.
Pillars of love, we build our home,
In every heart, we freely roam.

With kindness sewn through every seam,
We craft a life, we dream the dream.
Together strong, we face the days,
In understanding, we find our ways.

Echoes of Laughter

In the air, laughter rings bright,
Chasing shadows, bringing light.
Moments shared, a joyful sound,
In every corner, love is found.

The echoes dance through open fields,
In every heart, the smile yields.
A chorus sweet, memories blend,
In laughter's warmth, our spirits mend.

From whispered jokes to joyful screams,
We weave our days with silly dreams.
With every giggle, we rise anew,
A bond unbroken, ever true.

Through clouds of doubt, we find our cheer,
In every moment, hold it dear.
Echoes linger, floating free,
In laughter's embrace, we come to be.

As seasons pass, our joy remains,
In every smile, love still sustains.
With echoes soft, we find our way,
In laughter's arms, we choose to stay.

The Warmth of Presence

In quiet moments, shadows blend,
A sigh of solace, hearts extend.
Soft whispers linger, spirits dance,
Together we rise, in this chance.

Reach out, embrace the light we share,
In gentle glances, love laid bare.
Through trials faced, we stay resolved,
In this warm glow, we are absolved.

The laughter echoes, memories sway,
Holding hands as night meets day.
With every heartbeat, feelings ignite,
In the warmth of presence, we find light.

A tapestry spun with threads sincere,
Crafted by moments we hold dear.
Together we weather, storm and sun,
In this sacred space, we are one.

As years unfold, our stories grow,
In the warmth of presence, love will flow.
With every heartbeat, side by side,
With you, my heart forever bides.

Shared Dreams

Under the stars, our hopes take flight,
In whispered secrets, soft and light.
Together we forge a world so bright,
In the embrace of the endless night.

We paint our visions, colors bold,
Stories of laughter, adventures told.
With every sunrise, new paths emerge,
In the fabric of dreams, we converge.

In quiet moments, visions bloom,
A canvas alive, dispelling gloom.
With love as our guide, we navigate,
In shared dreams, we celebrate.

Through every challenge, hand in hand,
In unison, we make our stand.
With every heartbeat, futures weave,
In this world together, we believe.

Through night and day, our aspirations soar,
In the garden of dreams, we explore.
With every breath, our spirits gleam,
In the magic of life, we share our dream.

Lifelines Woven

Threads intertwine, a bond so strong,
Through joy and sorrow, we belong.
In moments fleeting, we find our way,
With lifelines woven, come what may.

A tapestry rich, with colors bright,
Each stitch a tale, a guiding light.
Through storms we weather, together we stand,
With lifelines woven, heart in hand.

In whispered vows, our fates align,
We share our dreams, our hopes entwine.
With every heartbeat, we draw near,
In this sacred weave, we hold dear.

Through laughter shared and tears we shed,
In life's embrace, our spirits tread.
With every chapter, our stories blend,
Lifelines woven, until the end.

In the fabric of life, our threads unite,
In the warmth of love, we find our light.
With every heartbeat, through joy and pain,
Together we've woven love's sweet chain.

Anchors of Affection

In turbulent seas, we find our way,
With anchors set, we choose to stay.
Through waves that crash and storms that wail,
Our hearts entwined, we will not fail.

With steady hands, we hold each other,
In moments fleeting, sister and brother.
Together we weather, trials and strife,
Anchors of affection, the heart of life.

In laughter's echo, in silence shared,
Through every hurdle, we have dared.
With love as our compass, we navigate,
Anchors of affection, together we create.

Through twilight's glow and dawn's embrace,
In your warm gaze, I find my place.
With every heartbeat, our bond will grow,
Anchors of affection, love's steady flow.

As seasons change and years unfold,
In every story, our hearts are bold.
With steadfast love, we'll always shore,
Anchors of affection, forevermore.

Colors of Camaraderie

In vibrant hues our hearts converge,
With laughter bright, our spirits surge.
Together strong, we share the light,
In friendship's bond, our souls take flight.

Blues of trust and greens of grace,
Within these shades, we find our place.
A tapestry of moments shared,
In every color, love declared.

With reds of passion, bold and free,
And yellows warm like sun-kissed glee,
We paint our world with strokes so fine,
In camaraderie, our lives entwine.

Through storms of doubt, we hold on tight,
Each shade a vow, a beacon's light.
With every brush, our tales unfold,
In colors bright, our bond is told.

So let our palette always show,
The hues of friendship, bright and glow.
For in the art of being true,
We find the joy of me and you.

The Sunlit Path

A golden trail beneath the trees,
Whispers of wind, a gentle breeze.
With every step, the world awakes,
A journey born, a road it makes.

The sunlit glow on leaves so green,
Nature's beauty, pure and serene.
Each ray of light a guiding hand,
Together we walk, through the land.

The path unfolds 'neath skies of blue,
Every moment, feels fresh and new.
With hearts aligned, we move as one,
Chasing dreams beneath the sun.

In laughter shared, in memories bright,
We trace our steps, igniting light.
Eclipsed by shadows, we'll stand tall,
Embracing sunlight, we won't fall.

So let us roam this sunlit way,
With open hearts, come what may.
For on this path, our spirits dance,
In every step, a new romance.

Meshing Melodies

In harmony our voices blend,
A symphony where dreams ascend.
Each note a story, sweet and clear,
Together strong, we sing with cheer.

The rhythm flows, a gentle stream,
In every beat, we find our dream.
With hearts attuned, we celebrate,
In shared melodies, we navigate.

Strumming chords of joy and pain,
Through each refrain, our love remains.
As whispers join in joyous flight,
We craft a song that feels just right.

The dance of sound, the pulse of life,
Together here, beyond the strife.
With every harmony, bonds we weave,
In music's warmth, we truly believe.

So let our melodies take wing,
In perfect time, together we sing.
For in this choir, hand in hand,
We find a world, so sweetly planned.

Resilient Roots

From silent depths, our courage sprouts,
Through rocky paths, and heavy doubts.
With every storm, we bend but don't break,
In nature's arms, new strength we make.

Roots intertwined, we stand so tall,
Supporting each, we shan't let fall.
In fertile soil, our dreams ignite,
Fostering hope, we reach for light.

Through seasons' change, we adapt and grow,
In shared resilience, love will flow.
Withstanding trials, we find our way,
In unity's strength, we seize the day.

Our branches stretch to touch the skies,
With every leaf, a new surprise.
In nature's cradle, we find our truth,
In resilient roots, we cherish youth.

So let our spirits always strive,
In harmony, we will survive.
For from the earth, our hearts take flight,
In resilient roots, we shine so bright.

Embracing the Journey

In the morning light we rise,
With dreams that touch the skies.
Footsteps lead us through the days,
Guiding us in countless ways.

Through valleys deep and mountains high,
We learn to laugh, we learn to cry.
Each twist and turn, a chance to grow,
Embracing paths we do not know.

The heart whispers, listen close,
In every urge, we find our dose.
Moments precious, fleeting, rare,
The journey teaches, if we dare.

As seasons change, we gather round,
In love and joy, our roots are found.
Together we face storms and sun,
The journey shared is truly fun.

With each new dawn, a canvas bright,
We paint our stories, pure delight.
Embracing all that comes our way,
In the journey, we find our stay.

Shared Secrets

In whispers soft, the truth unfolds,
In hidden places, treasures told.
A glance, a sigh, a nod of trust,
In shared secrets, love is just.

Behind closed doors, our hearts exchange,
In laughter sweet, we find our range.
Unraveled threads of shadowed past,
In shared moments, bonds are cast.

With every word, a step we take,
In fragile dreams, our fear we stake.
Through vulnerability we grow,
In secrets shared, our spirits glow.

The world outside may never know,
The depths of love that ebb and flow.
For those in tune, the silence speaks,
In shared secrets, solace seeks.

So hold my hand, let's soar above,
In sacred spaces, we find love.
An oath to keep, we'll always share,
Together bound, beyond compare.

The Art of Support

In gentle hands, we find our strength,
A bond that stretches all its length.
Through storms we face, we stand as one,
In every battle, hope is spun.

A listening ear, a kind embrace,
In darkest hours, we find our grace.
With whispered words that heal our heart,
The art of support plays its part.

Each step we take, a dance of trust,
In every moment, we must adjust.
With eyes that see the hidden tears,
In strength we find, we conquer fears.

When one falls down, the other stays,
In unity, our spirits blaze.
Together flowing, like a stream,
The art of support fulfills the dream.

With love and care, we paint the way,
A masterpiece that will not fray.
In every heartbeat, strong and true,
The art of support is me and you.

A Canvas of Connections

On life's vast canvas, colors blend,
Each stroke of fate, a hand to lend.
In vibrant hues, our stories merge,
A tapestry where dreams emerge.

With every laugh, a shade of light,
In every tear, the colors bright.
Brushes dance with joy and pain,
In connections formed, we break the chain.

Together, we create a scene,
Of love and struggles, vibrant and keen.
In moments shared, the canvas grows,
A living art where friendship flows.

With hearts as palettes, bold and free,
Each friendship paints our destiny.
Through shadows deep and sunlight's glow,
A canvas of connections will always show.

So let us gather, hand in hand,
In this creation, we boldly stand.
Together, we'll explore and find,
A canvas of connections, intertwined.

In the Embrace of Trust

In shadows deep, we find the light,
A bond that's strong, through day and night.
With every word, we build a place,
In the embrace of trust, we find our grace.

Through storms that rage, we stand our ground,
In silent vows, our hearts are bound.
With open hands, we share our fear,
In the embrace of trust, we're always near.

Together we rise, together we fall,
In whispered hopes, we heed the call.
With courage fierce, we face the tide,
In the embrace of trust, we will abide.

As seasons change, our roots run deep,
In promises made, our dreams we keep.
In every challenge, we'll find the way,
In the embrace of trust, we'll never sway.

In laughter shared and tears let flow,
Through every path, together we go.
With hearts aligned, we'll find the key,
In the embrace of trust, we are free.

Lanterns of Hope

In darkest hours, we light the flames,
With lanterns bright, we call your names.
Through winding paths, and nights so long,
Our hearts united, in a hopeful song.

The flicker glows, a guiding star,
Each step we take, we're never far.
In shadows cast, we find our glow,
With lanterns of hope, we let love flow.

When storms arise, and doubts creep in,
We stand as one, and together we win.
In each small spark, a future shines,
With lanterns of hope, our fate entwines.

Through trial and pain, we'll light the way,
In every moment, come what may.
With courage bold, we face the night,
With lanterns of hope, we find our light.

Together we dream and dance through fear,
With lanterns of hope, our vision is clear.
In every heartbeat, a promise made,
With lanterns of hope, we'll never fade.

The Journey of Us

With every step, we forge our path,
In rhythms shared, we find our math.
A tapestry woven with threads so fine,
In the journey of us, our hearts align.

Through hills and valleys, side by side,
With open arms, we both confide.
In laughter's sound and whispers soft,
In the journey of us, we rise aloft.

Each stumble met with gentle grace,
In every challenge, we find our place.
With trust imparted, and love held tight,
In the journey of us, we ignite the night.

As seasons shift, and winds do change,
We build a love that won't grow strange.
In every moment, our souls connect,
In the journey of us, we both reflect.

Through dreams we chase, and hopes we share,
In every heartbeat, in tender care.
With hands entwined, we'll face the dawn,
In the journey of us, we carry on.

Voices in Unison

In harmony found, we rise as one,
With voices strong, till the day is done.
In every note, a story told,
Voices in unison, brave and bold.

Through trials faced, we sing our song,
With hearts united, we all belong.
In every chord, a hope that sings,
Voices in unison, love takes wing.

As rhythms dance, and passions flare,
In the silence felt, we find our care.
With every beat, our spirits soar,
Voices in unison, we want more.

Together we rise, a symphony bright,
In every shadow, we bring the light.
With shared dreams, our dreams are vast,
Voices in unison, hold me fast.

In the journey shared, we weave a tale,
With dreams that flourish and love that prevails.
In every heartbeat, a promise rings,
Voices in unison, the joy it brings.

Unspoken Understanding

In silence we find our peace,
Words unneeded, hearts will cease.
Glimpses shared with subtle grace,
An unwritten bond we trace.

Eyes that speak without a sound,
Moments linger, love profound.
Even in the quiet night,
Familiar warmth feels just right.

A knowing glance, a tender sigh,
No need for questions, no goodbyes.
In this space, we come alive,
A silent dance helps us thrive.

Threads of thought entwined as one,
We share shadows, touch the sun.
The world fades, it's just us here,
In this place, there's nothing to fear.

In unspoken ways, we find,
The deepest ties, two souls aligned.
A language forged in all we do,
Unwritten love feels always true.

Melodies of Mutuality

In harmony, our voices blend,
A symphony without an end.
Notes entwined, we find our song,
In perfect time where we belong.

Your laughter dances on the breeze,
Like whispers through the swaying trees.
In every moment, rhythms play,
Creating magic day by day.

Together, we compose the score,
Each heartbeat plays, we crave for more.
Our differences, a sweet refrain,
In melodies that ease our pain.

With every glance, a tune unfolds,
In shared stories, life retold.
Through trials faced and joys embraced,
Our music lingers, never spaced.

In these moments, love is clear,
With every note, you draw me near.
In unity, our hearts align,
As melodies of mutuality shine.

The Garden of Companionship

In fragrant blooms, together we grow,
Nurtured roots beneath the snow.
Hand in hand, we plant our seeds,
Tending dreams and cherished needs.

Sunlight dances on our days,
Gentle winds through verdant ways.
In whispers soft, we find our place,
The garden thrives in love's embrace.

Colorful petals, vibrant and bright,
Each memory blooms in warm sunlight.
Together, we weather any storm,
In nature's arms, we feel reborn.

Even when the seasons change,
In dark moments, we rearrange.
Through thorny paths, we stand our ground,
In this garden, peace is found.

Companionship, a fertile field,
With tender care, our hearts revealed.
In shared laughter, blossoms sigh,
Together, we'll reach for the sky.

Companions in Solitude

In quiet walks, we share our space,
Two shadows moving at a pace.
In solitude, we find our kin,
A tender bond, where we begin.

Amidst the stillness, hearts connect,
In whispered thoughts, we gently reflect.
The world outside may fade away,
But here with you, I choose to stay.

With every breath, the silence speaks,
In moments shared, our spirit peaks.
Together facing the unknown,
In solitude, we've clearly grown.

Through timeless hours, we discover,
In quietude, we're like no other.
In softness, we navigate the void,
In precious silence, love enjoyed.

As seasons change, our hearts remain,
Through solitude, we share the strain.
In the depths, it's you and me,
Companions found, forever free.

Embracing Diversity

In colors bright, we find our way,
Each story told, a new array.
Voices blend, a vibrant song,
Together we stand, where we belong.

From distant lands, our paths entwined,
With open hearts, we speak our minds.
Cultures rich, like threads in lace,
A tapestry of light we trace.

Differences spark a deeper hue,
A world more rich, a view anew.
We celebrate, we learn, we grow,
In every face, a friend we know.

United by the strength we share,
In every gesture, kindness rare.
Hand in hand, we break each wall,
Together we rise, together we call.

With every step, we understand,
A brighter future, hand in hand.
Embracing all that makes us free,
In unity, our harmony.

Unity in Diversity

In every heart, a different beat,
Together we dance, our spirits meet.
A shared journey, through joy and strife,
In diversity, we find new life.

From every shore, we greet the dawn,
Woven paths of lives reborn.
Errors forgiven, bridges built,
In unity, there lies no guilt.

Voices varied, a beautiful song,
In our differences, we all belong.
Colors blend, a vibrant swirl,
In this canvas, we all unfurl.

Together we stand, hand in hand,
A promise of peace across the land.
Through trials faced, we grow more strong,
In unity's grace, we shall belong.

With every smile, a bond held tight,
In our embrace, the future's bright.
Through thick and thin, we pave the way,
In unity, we work and play.

Hands Held High

With hands held high, we reach for the sky,
In unity's strength, we learn to fly.
Together we rise, against the tide,
With courage and hope, always our guide.

A circle formed, no one stands alone,
In embrace of warmth, we've brightly grown.
Voices raised, our anthem sings,
In every moment, love's joy it brings.

In every heart, a wish takes flight,
With hands held high, we claim our right.
Together we shine, a blazing light,
For hope and love, we stand upright.

Through storms that come, we stand our ground,
In every struggle, resilience found.
Bound by the dreams that fill our sky,
Together we stand, hands held high.

With every heartbeat, our pact remains,
In peace and purpose, we break the chains.
Hope in our grasp, the world will see,
Hand in hand, we strive to be free.

Silent Promises

In whispers soft, we weave our dreams,
Silent promises, like flowing streams.
Through hidden paths, our spirits soar,
In the quiet moments, we seek for more.

A glance exchanged, a bond grown deep,
In the still of night, our secrets keep.
With silent vows beneath the stars,
Together we heal, despite our scars.

Through gentle touch, we share our fears,
With open hearts, we dry our tears.
Silent promises, a sacred trust,
In every heartbeat, we know we must.

In laughter shared, in sorrow's grace,
Together we find our rightful place.
Though words may fail, our hearts will know,
Silent promises help us grow.

With time ahead, our journey's clear,
In every silence, you'll find me near.
Together we'll soar, in every breath,
With silent promises, defying death.

Pebbles on the Path

Pebbles lie scattered, soft and round,
Each one a story, waiting to be found.
Stepping carefully, we tread along,
Nature's small treasures, where we belong.

Beneath our feet, whispers of the past,
Echoing journeys, memories amassed.
Colors and textures in a gentle light,
Guiding our footsteps, morning to night.

With each gentle step, we feel the earth,
Reminders of moments, each with worth.
In silence we pause, to observe and see,
The beauty of life, simple and free.

A child's laughter, a heart set aglow,
Pebbles ignite joy, far and near to show.
From distant hills to the riverside,
Nature's small wonders, our hearts confide.

As the sun sets low, shadows stretch long,
Our journey continues, with hope and song.
Together we wander, hand in hand by chance,
Pebbles on the path, life's sweet dance.

A Dance of Hearts

In a crowded room, eyes softly meet,
A spark ignites, a heartbeat's sweet beat.
Rhythm of souls in delicate tune,
A dance begins beneath the soft moon.

Hands intertwine, a gentle embrace,
Lost in the moment, in love's sacred space.
Whispers of dreams shared under the stars,
Two beating hearts, no distance too far.

With every twirl, the world fades away,
Footsteps of passion lead night into day.
Laughter and smiles, the music we find,
In this dance of hearts, souls are entwined.

A fleeting glance, a promise unspoken,
In this rhythm, no heart goes broken.
Together they sway in life's gentle flow,
A dance of hearts, where love's light will glow.

As dawn breaks softly, the dance carries on,
With courage and warmth, they greet the new dawn.
In every heartbeat, in whispers of art,
They'll forever remember this dance of hearts.

Elements of Empathy

A whisper of wind through branches sways,
Tells us of stories from faraway days.
In each soft rustle, compassion's sweet call,
Embracing the world, we rise, we fall.

The warmth of the sun, gentle and bright,
Cascading kindness, dispelling the night.
With each golden ray, we learn to believe,
In the strength of our hearts, the love we weave.

Raindrops embrace petals, a tender caress,
Washing away sorrow, bringing the bless.
In puddles we laugh, our spirits set free,
Finding connections in all that we see.

Each element speaks, a lesson to share,
The depths of our being, laid tender and bare.
In fire's warm glow, we gather and mend,
Building bridges of trust, hand in hand, friends.

As the moonlight bathes the world in dreams,
We rise together, united at seams.
Empathy blooms, a garden of grace,
In the elements' dance, we find our place.

Chasing Shadows Together

In the fading light, shadows start to dance,
We chase their forms, caught in the romance.
Hand in hand, we wander, hearts wide and free,
With laughter and dreams, just you and me.

Through fields of gold, where the sun dips low,
We race with the shadows, our faces aglow.
Every leap and bound draws us ever near,
In this playful chase, there is nothing to fear.

Whispers of twilight weave stories so bright,
As we move through dusk, into the night.
With moonbeams to guide us, we'll never tire,
Casting our own spell, woven in fire.

Together, we sketch silhouettes in the air,
Tracing our dreams, each moment we share.
Forever we'll chase, with no end in sight,
In the dance of shadows, everything feels right.

As stars appear, our hearts sync, align,
In this magical journey, love's grand design.
Chasing shadows together, side by side,
In the realm of the night where dreams abide.

Silent Promises

In the hush of twilight's glow,
Whispers linger, soft and low.
Hearts embrace unspoken words,
Bound by dreams, like nesting birds.

Echoes through the silent night,
Promises that feel just right.
In the shadows, hope shall bloom,
Filling spaces, dispelling gloom.

Time may stretch and often bend,
Yet these vows will never end.
Under stars, we find our way,
Silent truths that gently sway.

With each breath, our souls align,
Crafting love that's pure, divine.
Though the world around may change,
Your heart stays, eternally strange.

As the dawn begins to rise,
Revealing warmth in painted skies.
Silent promises we keep,
Awake, alive, not lost in sleep.

Bridges Over Time

Span the rivers, forge the ties,
In moments lost, connection lies.
To futures bright and pasts so dear,
We build the bridges, year by year.

Through seasons' shift, our hearts remain,
Navigating joy and pain.
On sturdy beams, we walk as one,
Embracing sights of day begun.

Each step echoes stories shared,
Of love and trust, forever paired.
Through storms that try to tear apart,
We hold the strands that bind the heart.

As twilight paints the sky with dreams,
We traverse the gentle streams.
In bonds of gold, we find our rhyme,
Eternal paths, through space and time.

With every crossing, souls ignite,
Guiding us through day and night.
Together, strong, we face the climb,
Building bridges, transcending time.

Harmonies of Shared Dreams

In the quiet, voices blend,
A symphony that has no end.
Each note a wish, a hope, a prayer,
Echoing love that we both share.

Like gentle waves, our dreams take flight,
Crashing softly in the night.
Together, we create the song,
In perfect harmony, we belong.

Melodies flow in intertwined fates,
A dance of laughter that never waits.
Through trials faced, we find our tune,
An opus shining like the moon.

Through every trial, we find a beat,
With each heartbeat, our lives complete.
In this chorus, joy prevails,
As our shared story gently sails.

With every sunset, new dreams arise,
Painting futures across the skies.
In the echoes of our refrain,
Lives our love, our sweetest gain.

Tapestry of Kinship

Threads of life, woven tight,
Colors bright, a pure delight.
In every strand, a story lies,
Kinsfolk gathered 'neath the skies.

Each pattern marks a bond we share,
Moments cherished, love laid bare.
In laughter and in gentle tears,
We weave our joy throughout the years.

Through seasons' change, our fibers blend,
Crafting warmth that will not end.
In trials faced, we stand as one,
Together shining like the sun.

A tapestry of hearts so bold,
Woven tales of warmth unfold.
With every knot, our trust remains,
Holding strong through joys and pains.

In the patterns, history shows,
A love that in the silence grows.
Forever stitched, we find our way,
In this kinship, come what may.

Heartstrings Entwined

In the quiet hours of night,
Whispers dance in gentle light.
Fingers trace the silver thread,
Binding hearts where love is led.

Beneath the stars, two souls align,
Every look, a secret sign.
Laughter echoes, softly spun,
Together, we are always one.

Time may wane, but bonds will grow,
Feeling deep within the flow.
Every tear and every smile,
Weaving dreams, a sacred pile.

Through the storms and sunny skies,
Always seeing through each other's eyes.
Hand in hand, we take the flight,
In our hearts, a lasting light.

As seasons change and shadows fall,
We'll rise above, we'll never stall.
Two heartstrings, forever twined,
In the depths, true love defined.

Alchemy of Trust

In the furnace of the soul,
Faith ignites, making us whole.
Every secret shared a gem,
Polished bright, a rare diadem.

Like the phoenix from the flame,
Trust transforms, never the same.
Turning fears into pure gold,
In this bond, we become bold.

Each promise made, a sacred pact,
In the silence, we both act.
Walk with me through shadowed nights,
In our hearts, forever light.

Through the storms, we build a wall,
Rooted deep, we never fall.
Alchemy of souls entwined,
In this love, true peace we find.

With every breath, the magic flows,
In trust's garden, our love grows.
Hand in hand, we face the light,
Together, we'll win the fight.

The Unseen Bridge

Across the void, a whisper calls,
An echo in the empty halls.
With every heartbeat, I take flight,
On the bridge of love, all feels right.

Invisible, yet power strong,
Each glance, we've known all along.
Through the distance, hearts can soar,
Building pathways, craving more.

When silence wraps the world in gray,
This bridge, our guide, will light the way.
In the dreams where we unite,
We find each other, pure delight.

Though miles stretch like endless sea,
In our hearts, we always flee.
Connected by invisible string,
On this bridge, our spirits sing.

Time will test, yet we will stand,
Stronger still, hand in hand.
Through life's journey, we will roam,
On this bridge, we've found our home.

Seasons of Connection

In springtime's bloom, our laughter rings,
Life awakens as the heart sings.
Petals falling, colors bright,
Moments crafted, pure delight.

Summer days with golden rays,
In your gaze, the world ablaze.
Warmth surrounding, love's embrace,
Within your arms, I find my place.

As autumn paints with strokes of fire,
Leaves drift down, hearts never tire.
Every rustle, every sigh,
Seasons change, yet we comply.

In winter's chill, we find the flame,
Through frosty nights, we're not the same.
Holding close, our shadows blend,
In this warmth, our hearts mend.

Through each season, time flows on,
Moments cherished, never gone.
Together, we embrace the bend,
In every change, love's the thread.

Compass Points of Connection

In the north, we find our way,
Guided by the stars that sway.
In the east, the dawn breaks clear,
Filling hearts with light and cheer.

In the south, the warmth will glow,
Where friendships flourish, hearts aglow.
In the west, the sun sets low,
Reminds us of the love we sow.

Together we chart our course,
With every bond, we find our source.
Through storms and calm, we navigate,
Each point a thread that ties our fate.

In laughter and in whispered dreams,
We forge our paths through life's extremes.
Compass points, a guiding hand,
In unity, we always stand.

So let the winds of fate align,
In every heart, your truth will shine.
With each connection, we will grow,
Compass points, our love will show.

Whispered Secrets

In shadows deep, the secrets dwell,
Soft whispers weave their magic spell.
With every sigh, the truth is spun,
In quiet corners, hearts are won.

Beneath the stars, we softly share,
A fragile bond, so pure and rare.
In gentle tones, the night unfolds,
Stories etched in dreams retold.

With rustling leaves, our secrets float,
On fleeting winds, like fragile notes.
In silent vows, our hopes align,
With every echo, love will shine.

The world may hush, but we will know,
In whispered words, our feelings grow.
Through every fear, our hearts will thaw,
Embracing truths, both weak and raw.

So let your voice be soft and true,
In whispered secrets, I find you.
In every hush, our souls connect,
In tender moments, we reflect.

A Dance of Souls

In twilight's embrace, we find our rhythm,
Two souls entwined, lost in the vision.
With every step, our hearts align,
In this dance, a love divine.

Under moonlight, we spin and sway,
In gentle currents, we drift away.
With every twirl, our spirits soar,
In this ballet, we crave for more.

Through laughter's notes and silent sighs,
We lose ourselves where beauty lies.
Every glance, a spark ignites,
A dance of souls, where love excites.

In the stillness, our dreams take flight,
Guided by stars, we chase the night.
With every beat, our hearts collide,
In this cherished dance, we confide.

So let the music play its tune,
In every tone, our souls commune.
Together we waltz, side by side,
In this dance of love, we shall abide.

Growing in the Light

From seeds of hope, we rise and bloom,
In the light, we dispel the gloom.
With every ray, our spirits thrive,
In warmth and love, we come alive.

Through seasons' change, we nurture care,
In gentle hands, we find our share.
With roots that anchor deep and strong,
In unity, we all belong.

The sun ignites our passion bright,
As shadows fade, we soar in flight.
In every challenge, we will grow,
With love and kindness, let it flow.

Through gentle rains and winds that pause,
We flourish on, for love's the cause.
Together in this bond we weave,
In light and joy, we shall believe.

So cherish the moments, hold them tight,
In every heart, we find the light.
As flowers bloom and spirits sing,
Together, in the light, we'll spring.

Echoing Hearts

In whispers soft, we find our way,
Two souls entwined, in night and day.
Each heartbeat sings a gentle tune,
In echoes rich beneath the moon.

With every step, our shadows blend,
Through laughter shared, we start to mend.
The world's vast space, yet here we stand,
United close, hand in hand.

Through trials faced and fences crossed,
In knowing hearts, we count our cost.
Each moment's grace, a treasure dear,
In echoes clear, our love draws near.

Through winding paths and restless tide,
Our spirits soar, their wings opened wide.
In every glance, a flame ignites,
In echoes soft, love's warmth excites.

So let us dance in twilight's glow,
With hearts aflame, we'll rise and flow.
In echoes sweet, our journey starts,
Together strong, echoing hearts.

Anchors in the Storm

When howling winds begin to roar,
And darkened skies loom evermore,
We find our strength, we stand as one,
Through raging waves, our hearts undone.

With every storm, we hold our ground,
In steadfast love, our hope is found.
Like anchors deep, we won't be swayed,
In tempest's grip, our bond displayed.

The lightning strikes but lights the way,
Through trials faced, we won't delay.
With every drop, a lesson learned,
In storm's embrace, our passion burned.

And when the clouds begin to clear,
We'll hold each other, calm our fear.
With shimmering rainbows in the sky,
As anchors strong, we'll rise and fly.

In perfect sync, we brave the night,
With hearts aligned, we shine so bright.
Through all the storms that life may bring,
We are the anchors, love's sweet ring.

Celebrating Differences

In colors bright, we paint the scene,
A canvas rich, where hearts convene.
Each voice unique, a song to share,
In differences, we find our flair.

With open arms, we greet the day,
In laughter, joy, and bright array.
No one the same, yet all belong,
Together strong, we rise in song.

From every tale, a lesson drawn,
In varied paths, through dusk and dawn.
With hands held high and spirits free,
In differences, we find unity.

We celebrate the shades of life,
In every joy, in every strife.
With open hearts, we weave our thread,
In vibrant hues, our stories spread.

So let us dance in harmony,
Embracing all in unity.
For in each heart, a truth exists,
In celebrating, love persists.

Unbreakable Circles

In endless loops, our lives entwined,
In circles drawn, our hearts aligned.
A bond that stands through thick and thin,
In every loss, in every win.

With laughter shared, we build our space,
In trust and hope, we find our grace.
Together strong, we face the fight,
In unbreakable circles, love ignites.

Like rings of gold, our promise shines,
Through seasons changed and twisted lines.
We stand as one, a steadfast crew,
In every challenge, we break through.

As time moves on, the world may sway,
But in this circle, we'll always stay.
With arms held wide and spirits high,
In unbreakable circles, we will fly.

So let us sing our songs of cheer,
In every heart, love's echo clear.
In circles round, our truth proclaims,
Unbreakable bonds, forever flames.

Shared Moments

In the quiet of the night,
We hear whispers of the stars,
Time pauses, holding tight,
To the dreams we share, not far.

Laughter dances in the air,
Like fireflies in gentle flight,
Every glance, a treasured flare,
Illuminating joy's pure light.

With every step, we create
Memories etched in our minds,
Time's embrace, we celebrate,
Together, all that love finds.

In a world that spins so fast,
We find solace in the slow,
These moments, destined to last,
As our hearts gently glow.

Through a storm or sunshine's chase,
Hand in hand, we journey bold,
In the warmth of our embrace,
Life's tapestry unfolds.

Shared Hearts

Two souls dance in sweet refrain,
Beats entwined, a rhythmic flow,
Through joy's laughter and through pain,
Our hearts speak what words can't show.

When shadows loom and doubts arise,
We lean on love's steadfast grace,
With each tear and with each sigh,
We find strength in our shared space.

In quiet moments, soft and near,
A glance can say what lips can't say,
In the silence, we persevere,
Connected in every way.

With open hearts, we build our song,
Each note a promise, pure and true,
In this journey, we belong,
Wrapped in love's vibrant hue.

Through storms we brave, we rise anew,
With courage, hand in hand we stand,
In shared hearts, our dreams come true,
Together, a united band.

Ties that Bind

Threads of laughter woven tight,
A tapestry of moments grand,
In shared joys, our spirits light,
Building dreams with gentle hands.

When the road grows dark and steep,
In our hearts, a lantern glows,
Through the valleys, wide and deep,
Love's pure bond forever flows.

In the dance of life, we sway,
Guided by a shared heartbeat,
Finding strength in every day,
As our paths continuously meet.

What we share is more than gold,
It's trust and laughter intertwined,
In our stories, bright and bold,
The ties that bind are love defined.

With every trial, hand in hand,
We weather storms, we warm the nights,
Together, united we stand,
In love's embrace, our hearts ignite.

Canvas of Companionship

With colors bright, our lives unfold,
Strokes of love and laughter blend,
On this canvas, tales are told,
In every hue, our hearts extend.

Brush of kindness, touch of care,
Layering dreams in vibrant tones,
In the silence, we both share,
A masterpiece, love's soft moans.

Through the storms, we paint our skies,
With every splash, our spirits soar,
In the depths of each sunrise,
We find beauty to explore.

In every shadow, a story laid,
With light and dark, we find our way,
In this art, our hearts displayed,
A bond that never fades away.

Together, we create our scene,
In the gallery of our days,
With each moment, bold and keen,
Our love is the masterpiece that stays.

Navigating Together

In the journey, hand in hand,
Charting stars on skies so wide,
Through the seas, we make our stand,
As compass guides, love's trust our tide.

Every wave, a lesson learned,
Every shore, a tale to tell,
In this adventure, hearts have yearned,
Navigating life, under love's spell.

Through the storms that howl and roar,
We find calm in our embrace,
With every challenge faced, we soar,
Together, we create our space.

Each landmark marks our growth and change,
With laughter echoing in the air,
Though paths may twist and sometimes range,
In our hearts, we hold the dare.

This voyage, rich with dreams and hope,
With every turn, our spirits rise,
Together, we learn how to cope,
Hand in hand, beneath vast skies.

Shelters from the Storm

In the heart of chaos, we find our place,
Amidst the gusts, our souls embrace.
With sheltering arms and whispers soft,
Together we rise, no matter the cost.

Clouds may darken, shadows may fight,
But love is our beacon, a guiding light.
With laughter and warmth, we weather the night,
In each other's presence, we hold on tight.

Through tempest and turmoil, we stand as one,
Facing the fury till the morning sun.
With faith in our hearts, we'll stand strong and tall,
In the eye of the storm, we won't let each fall.

Let the rain pour down, let the thunder roar,
In our little haven, we'll find much more.
For every storm fades, giving way to grace,
We'll dance in the sun, in our sacred space.

So here in this shelter, with you, I stay,
Together we conquer, come what may.
For every dark moment, there's light to reclaim,
Our love is the shelter, our hearts the same.

Lanterns of Light

In the silence of night, hope flickers bright,
Each lantern a promise, a guiding light.
We wander together, hand in hand,
Through shadows and doubts, in this vast land.

With whispers of dreams, our spirits take flight,
Chasing the stars, painting the night.
Each glow tells a story, each flame a song,
In unity's warmth, we find where we belong.

Through trials we face, the path may seem long,
But with lanterns alight, we can't go wrong.
With laughter and courage, we illuminate,
The corners of darkness, we navigate.

So cherish these moments, these flickering sights,
For love is the lantern that banishes fright.
In the depths of our hearts, we carry the glow,
Together we shine, as we let love flow.

In the stillness of twilight, let our hopes rise,
With lanterns of light, we embrace the skies.
For every lost soul, may we be their guide,
Together we brighten, with hearts open wide.

Notes of Understanding

In the symphony of life, we write our score,
With notes of compassion, we yearn for more.
With each gentle chord, we bridge the divide,
Finding harmony, with hearts open wide.

Words intertwined, like a soft gentle breeze,
In the dance of our thoughts, we find our peace.
Through laughter and sorrow, we make our blend,
These notes carry stories, where hearts can mend.

With every shared silence, we listen and learn,
In the warmth of connection, our passions burn.
Together we chart, this unspoken art,
With notes of understanding that echo the heart.

So here's to our journey, to growth and to trust,
For in every moment, we cherish and adjust.
With every kind word, a melody plays,
Bringing colors of joy to our endless days.

As we write our own verses, hand in hand we stand,
Creating a symphony across this land.
With notes that uplift, may we rise and soar,
In the music of life, we find so much more.

Reflections of Us

In the mirror of time, what do we see?
Reflections of moments, you and me.
With laughter and tears, we've weathered the years,
Through every heartbeat, we conquer our fears.

Like echoes of laughter, our stories entwine,
In the tapestry woven, your heart next to mine.
Together we wander, through shadows and light,
In the depths of our bond, we shine ever bright.

Each glance a reminder, of paths we have crossed,
In the light of our love, there's never a loss.
With whispers of dreams, we carve our own way,
In reflections of us, come what may.

With every shared moment, we build and we grow,
In the mirror of love, our true selves we show.
These reflections, a testament, to all we've achieved,
In each other's arms, we've always believed.

So here's to the journey, the bond that we share,
In the reflections of us, a love that is rare.
With every heartbeat, we write our own song,
In the mirror of time, where our hearts belong.

A Quilt of Kindness

In every stitch, a story sewn,
Threads of compassion softly grown.
Colors blend, a warm embrace,
A patchwork of love in every place.

Hands create what hearts design,
Kind gestures in this pattern divine.
Each square a moment shared in grace,
A quilt of kindness time can't erase.

When troubles loom, it wraps us tight,
A shield against the dark of night.
Within its folds, we find our way,
A beacon bright that guides our stay.

Through laughter loud and whispers low,
This tapestry of care will grow.
We gather strength from those we know,
In every patch, our spirits flow.

So spread this quilt where shadows fall,
Let love and kindness speak for all.
Together stitching dreams anew,
A quilt that binds me close to you.

Radiant Reflections

In still waters, truths reside,
Mirrors of the heart, open wide.
Glimmers dance on surfaces clear,
Whispers of love, so sincere.

Echoes of laughter paint the scene,
Moments cherished, vibrant and keen.
Sunlight filters through the trees,
In nature's calm, our spirits ease.

Every ripple tells a tale,
Of dreams that dared to set the sail.
Gazing deep, we find our way,
In radiant light, we choose to stay.

A canvas where our souls collide,
Reflections speak, we cannot hide.
In the quiet, truths unfurl,
Together in this wondrous swirl.

Caught in moments, pure and rare,
Life's reflections beyond compare.
We journey forth, hearts intertwined,
In every glance, our love defined.

Dance of Devotion

In twilight's glow, we find our grace,
A gentle leap, a sweet embrace.
Step by step, our spirits rise,
In rhythm with the starlit skies.

Twirls of joy, in laughter's sway,
In each heartbeat, we find our way.
A melody that fills the air,
In every glance, a silent prayer.

Through every trial, we hold on tight,
In the dance of love, we ignite.
United steps, both strong and free,
In perfect harmony, you and me.

With every note, our passions flow,
Graceful movements, a cherished show.
In devotion's embrace, we sway,
Together forever, come what may.

So let the music take the lead,
In this dance, we plant the seed.
For love's rhythm, we will strive,
In this dance of devotion, we thrive.

Nurturing Nods

In gentle smiles, we find our peace,
With quiet nods, all worries cease.
A simple gesture, yet so profound,
In every look, a love unbound.

With open hearts, our kindness grows,
Reflections of the care we chose.
Through storms and sun, we stand as one,
In nurturing nods, our day is won.

Each shared glance a promise made,
In the tapestry of life, we braid.
With every acknowledgment true,
We weave a world made for me and you.

Through trials faced, we lift our eyes,
In the warmth of shared ties, we rise.
Together in this bond so tight,
Nurturing nods bring sheer delight.

So let us cherish every glance,
In love's embrace, we take our chance.
With hearts aligned and spirits free,
Nurturing nods, just you and me.

Hearts in Harmony

In the quiet of the night,
Two hearts beat as one,
Dancing to the soft sound,
Of love's sweet song begun.

With every whispered breath,
A promise softly made,
Guiding through the shadows,
In laughter, fears allayed.

Together we will wander,
Through paths both bright and dim,
Hand in hand, we'll conquer,
With love, our guiding hymn.

The world may be chaotic,
But here, we find our peace,
A symphony of heartbeats,
Where chaos finds release.

As starlight paints the sky,
Our dreams begin to soar,
With hearts in perfect sync,
Forever we will explore.

A Tapestry of Togetherness

Threads of gold and silver,
Woven tight with care,
In colors bold and gentle,
A tapestry we share.

Each moment spins a story,
Stitched with laughter's glow,
In this quilt of living,
Our bonds are all we know.

Through seasons that are changing,
We stand side by side,
In the warmth of our embrace,
Together as our guide.

The fabric of our journey,
Is rich with memories,
In the weave of moments shared,
Our love's sweet melodies.

With every stitch and pattern,
We craft a life so bright,
A tapestry of togetherness,
In the softest light.

The Ties That Bind

In the threads of our laughter,
A bond begins to form,
Woven through the heart,
Weathering every storm.

The echoes of our secrets,
In whispers softly spun,
Create a bridge of trust,
Where two become as one.

In the dance of togetherness,
We find our footing clear,
With steps that intertwine,
In love, there is no fear.

The ties that bind us closely,
Are stronger than the sea,
Through tides of life we journey,
Together, you and me.

As seasons shift and follow,
Our hearts stay intertwined,
In every thread we flourish,
In love we are defined.

Whispers of Companionship

In the stillness of the evening,
Soft whispers fill the air,
Promises and secrets,
Shared with loving care.

Through the trials we are facing,
A gentle hand to hold,
In the warmth of companionship,
Our stories will unfold.

With laughter as our beacon,
We travel on this road,
Two souls in perfect harmony,
Sharing each heavy load.

Through every joy and sorrow,
We find a brighter day,
In the whispers of companionship,
Love shows us the way.

Together we are stronger,
In every step we take,
With whispers of forever,
A bond that will not break.

Milton Keynes UK
Ingram Content Group UK Ltd.
UKHW022004131124
451149UK00013B/1006